Coloring book for adults and kids amazing rose image for design

This coloring book is belongs to

____

Freedom Rose

“ Roses ”

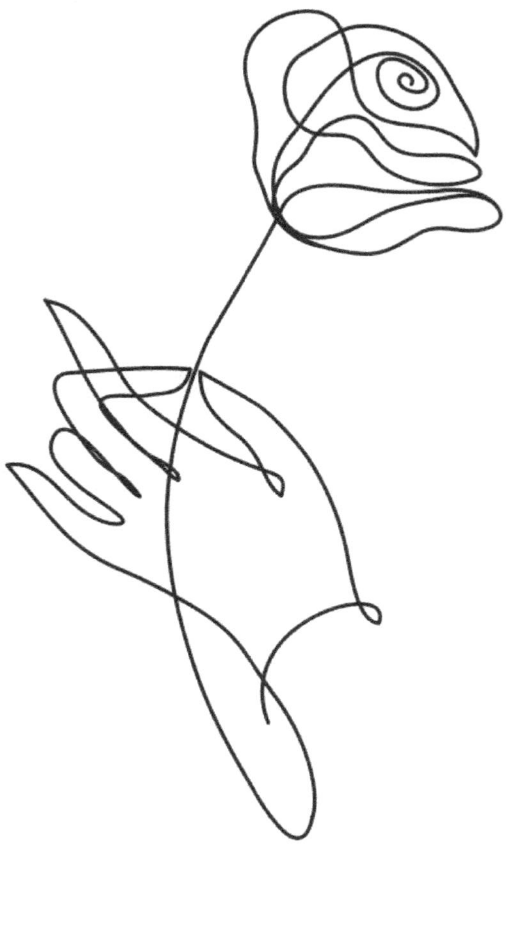

-RED ROSE-

Rose symbol collection

Beautiful roses
VECTOR

"WILD ROSE"

“WILD ROSE”

"WILD ROSE"

www.ingramcontent.com/pod-product-compliance
Lightning Source LLC
Chambersburg PA
CBHW081242250726
48654CB00012B/1449
* 9 7 9 8 7 0 5 1 9 7 7 8 1 *